I0177338

DEDICATION

To my mom, who has supported every dream I have ever had. And...

To every author who has ever had a Hollywood dream, you have the power to make it happen...

CONTENTS

RED
CARPET
MANUSCRIPT

HOW AUTHORS CAN BRING THEIR
BOOK TO THE BIG SCREEN

DR. ROB CARPENTER

Red Carpet Manuscript

Copyright © 2022 Dr. Rob Carpenter.
All Rights Reserved.

No part of this publication may be reproduced, stored in a retrieval system ortransmitted, in any form or by any eans—electronic, mechanical, photocopying, recording, or otherwise—without prior written permissionfrom the publisher, except for the inclusion of brief quotations in a review.

RMC Lit
New York, New York

ISBN: 978-1-7366155-4-6 (print)
ISBN: 978-1-7366155-5-3 (eBook)

For information about this title or for bulk orders, email books@DrRob.TV.

CHAPTER I

INTRODUCTION

"Don't ever let someone tell you you can't do something."

—*The Pursuit of Happyness*

I wrote this book so that you, the author— the HERO of this publication—could know exactly what to do to take your book, short story, trilogy series, article, or other piece of Intellectual Property (IP) and turn it into a movie or television show.

I wrote it because I realized that there are very few, if any, step-by-step manuals that show indie or traditionally published authors how to do this.

And I wrote it because I wanted to dispel the myth that you have to be a *New York Times* or *USA Today* bestseller, that you have to know somebody in Hollywood, or that you have to be "lucky" to somehow get a shot at getting your creation on screen for millions to see.

Ultimately, I wrote this book so that you, our HERO, could have a roadmap to empower yourself with the "specifics" and "particulars" of Hollywood so that you could start playing in the sandbox of Tinseltown.

Even if you only have modest book sales, live nowhere near Los Angeles, or currently have limited knowledge about what it takes to be successful in television and motion pictures, I wrote this book to show you that you can still move forward and see your movie and television dreams come true despite if others tell you that the the odds are against you.

But even if you personally feel like the odds are not in your favor I would caution you not to consider them. But why?

Because you didn't consider the odds when you decided to write your book or create your IP (something that millions of people want to do but have never done). If you looked at the odds, you probably wouldn't have ever gotten started—or finished—with your project. In other words, you are already a person who has proven they can overcome the odds (as tough as the odds may have been) and so they don't apply to you the way they might apply to others. As they say, luck favors the bold (and you, my friend, are the bold).

The one thing I would suggest to you is not to consider the odds but to instead consider whether you want to try to make your dreams come true or not. Because in the best case scenario, you will achieve your Hollywood goal and wonder why you didn't do it sooner. You will see your work optioned (more on this later in the book), your book adapted to a screenplay, your favorite actors and director attached, and a marketing machine pushing the characters and the world you created. In a nutshell, you will see magic happen and you will wake up pinching yourself still not believing that you're living in a fairy tale.

But on the other hand, in the worst case scenario—not seeing things work out for you or your IP in the short run—you will learn a lot more than you ever knew before, meet new people, and can always try again with your next book or project. After all, sometimes you hit it big on your first book (like author Lauren Weisberger's debut book *The Devil Wears Prada*) but sometimes it takes a few tries (like author Suzanne Collins who didn't get her first shot at the big screen until her sixth published book *The Hunger Games*).

But regardless of whether you hit it big on your first attempt— or your sixth—the important thing is that you try. Of course, nothing is guaranteed in life or Hollywood but that doesn't mean that you can't get yourself closer to achieving the results you want once you understand the process you need to go through to be successful. That is, it doesn't mean that you can't get yourself closer to the results you want once you understand the "hidden formula" the insiders use to get things done to bring the world the movies and shows it craves.

I wrote this book to show you this "hidden formula" because I was disappointed in the usual advice I heard given to authors who want to get their work adapted. This advice typically goes something like this:

> To get your work adapted, all you have to do is hit a typical bestseller list—or the top 1% on Amazon if you're an indie author—and hope a producer contacts you.

While this contains elements of the truth, it is only the partial truth. And partial truth is actually just a little white lie wrapped in a bow tie that is holding you back from living your dreams.

Unfortunately, this partial truth is not really sound advice because it tells you that you are powerless as an author and that you have absolutely no control over being able to influence whether your IP becomes something big. This is simply not true. I repeat: this is simply not true.

Not only have I personally optioned books that were not best sellers in my producer capacity, many other producers have too. But why? Because not every project needs to be based on a bestseller list to be a high quality project. Of course it helps in certain cases with certain producers and studios to be on these lists, but it is neither necessary nor sufficient for every producer or studio (or movie or television project). And more and more, producers and studios are beginning to look to non-traditional—or new or hidden or unrepresented—authors because their work can be just as valuable as the big names when it comes to mining the IP gold these rising stars have created.

Who Am I To Write This Book

But who am I to give you any kind of guidance? The funny thing is not only am I an author and IP rights holder just like you, but I am also a film director, producer, screenwriter, and host who has spent years working inside—and learning—the entertainment business. I've been a filmmaker at the 2x Emmy Award winning USC Media Institute for Social Change, for example; am producing partners with an Academy Award winner; and have created and/or worked on shows in various stages of development with the major studios. Put simply, I love authors, I love movies and television, and I love all aspects of the entertainment industry and my life and career reflect this.

But in addition to my love for and experience being an author and working in Hollywood, I also consider myself a teacher. In fact, I have been a university professor and have taught courses, presented at, or written for institutions like Harvard University, Oxford University, and countless others. I have always enjoyed breaking down for others the "how" of something or showing them the "way" especially if it initially seems murky or uncertain for them. And I hope that I can do the same for you here.

Huge Demand For Your IP From Hollywood

Of course, we all know that Hollywood loves good books (like yours). Since the beginning of the industry, for example, Tinseltown has hungered over material to base books on. Films ranging from *It's A Wonderful Life* to *Gone with the Wind* to *The Avengers* have all been based on books —or even based on unpublished manuscripts that were not even "books" before they started to be turned into movies (as in the case of *It's a Wonderful Life*, which was an unpublished manuscript when it got the greenlight from Hollywood).

In fact, over 70% of all of the top grossing films in history have been based on books or unpublished manuscripts that are about to become books. And increasingly, more and more television shows are being based on books too. *Game of Thrones*, *Sharp Objects*, and *Little Fires Everywhere*, for example, have all come to the small screen after originating in a book. Given this phenomenon, over 50% of all television shows are now based on books or other types of IP—with this number growing on a daily basis.

As a consequence, all of the major traditional publishing houses— Simon & Schuster, Penguin/Random House, Harper Collins, Hachette, and Macmillan—all have agents (called "media rights" agents) who have developed relationships with Hollywood producers, agents, and studios to funnel them books they think could be the next big show or movie.

But where does that leave you, our HERO, if you are either not published by one of these groups or (if you are published by one of them) not referred to the Hollywood machine by your publishing house?

You Still Have A Chance

Even if you are not currently a part of the entertainment industry system, that is no reason to give up on your dream of seeing your work on the big or small screen. In fact, you should actually be encouraged because there has never been more opportunity than today to join this industry if you are willing to learn, be teachable, and believe in yourself and your own creative work. Right now, tens of billions of dollars are being spent on a content war in Hollywood and as a consequence it is looking everywhere for material—so it might as well be looking for (and buying) your work. After all, Hollywood has made indie books like *Legally Blonde*, *The Martian*, *Eragon*, and *Infinite* into huge on-screen hits so there is no reason it shouldn't do the same for your work.

In the pages that follow, I will try to as clearly and concisely as possible lay out the process of what you need to do to break into Hollywood as an indie or traditionally published author so you can tap into its ever growing opportunities; provide you with example documents you will need to create to get your foot in the door; explain the "business" side of how show business works for authors and the roles of the people you will be working with; give you specific strategies and tactics for how to reach busy producers, managers, and agents; and present next steps and additional opportunities you can use to accelerate your odds of success and get "insider access."

So buckle up, HERO, I'm going to show you the roadmap you can use to put yourself in the best position to make your Hollywood dreams come true.

CHAPTER 2

THE RIGHT MINDSET TO PLAY THE HOLLYWOOD GAME

> "At some point you've got to decide for yourself who you're gonna be, can't let anybody make that decision for you."
>
> — *Moonlight*

You Must Play The Game In Order To Win It

Hollywood is like a professional sports league. It is full of individual players (i.e., actors, writers, directors, etc.); individual teams (i.e., production companies, talent agencies, etc.); individual owners (i.e., studios, streamers, etc.); individual media commentators (i.e., publicists, celebrity and entertainment journalists, etc.); and more. Just like the NBA, MLB, or NFL.

Individual players are constantly jumping from team to team, for example, and owners are constantly adjusting their own rosters to offer better and better products (i.e., better shows and movies) to make more and more money.

Commentators document their every move trying to get a breaking news story or, at the very least, a little bit of click bait so they can make their own money.

And fans sit back in awe—and sometimes in frustration—as it all plays out in front of the world.

From the outside looking in, as an author—and as the newest HERO to enter the Hollywood system—all of this could leave you with lots of mixed emotions. On the one hand, it is incredibly exciting to audition your book to enter this league so that you too can play the game.

On the other hand, though, it might seem overwhelming with where you should start, who you should talk to, and how you can stand out in an industry that employs more than 600,000 people in front of and behind the scenes. After all, it seems like a glitzy (and noisy) machine with lots of locked gates and gatekeepers.

But while it might be all of these things, please remember this: all of these gates have keys that unlock them. And many of these gatekeepers will let you in if you know the right combination or password.

In other words, as our HERO I don't want you to think of Hollywood so much as a "closed system" looking to keep you out; I want you to think of it as a place full of many people just like you and me who want to help get you in so that you can succeed on your journey so long as you play the game the right way.

And by playing the game the right way I don't mean you have to lose your ethics or become a different person (you should never listen to anyone who tells you to do that). By playing the game the right way I mean you have to 1) have the right mindset for the game; 2) understand the culture of the game; and 3) understand what 'winning' a game looks like.

The Right Mindset For The Game

Having the right mindset for the game means that you, our HERO, has to first believe that they can and will succeed. It means that you have to disregard the odds everyone says are against you. And it means that you have to develop an attitude of "I don't quit until I win."

If there is one approach that works more often than it does not in Hollywood, it is this one. As our HERO, you shouldn't stop until you reach your goal no matter how unlikely it is—and no matter how long it takes. You must consistently choose faith over fear because that is the only thing that can never be taken from you in this industry (if you refuse to not let it be taken from you). Series and movies like *Mad Men* and *Gemini Man* took years and even decades to make, respectively, so having a long-term perspective and oodles of patience are required (even if not every project takes as long as these ones did).

Understanding The Culture Of The Game

Of course, you should couple the right mindset for the game with understanding its culture too. The culture of the game consists of knowing that it is made up of lots of different kinds of personality types, lots of different players at various levels of success, and an ever-changing business (and artistic) model that shifts people's fortunes (and misfortunes) quickly.

For example, a prominent actor or writer in vogue today could easily be replaced tomorrow by an unknown actor or writer who is not. A powerful producer today could be outshined (and dominated) by a new producer few are paying attention to. And a genre of television show or movie that is hot today could completely evaporate in favor of something entirely different tomorrow.

In other words, understanding the culture of the game is knowing that 1) the talent (and executives) are always changing; 2) the teams are always changing; 3) the winners are always changing; 4) the business models are always changing; and 5) nothing is ever permanent or final in Hollywood. Ever. This means that the industry could yawn at your IP today but literally get into a bidding war over it tomorrow (and I have personally seen this play out with my own work).

Having said that, this is especially why you should invest in relationships with players at all levels of the game who can help you reach your goals (whether in the short-term or the long-term). This means, as the HERO, not just talking to those players you perceive as "on top" now but talking to anybody else in the industry (who seems credible) too. In practical terms, this can mean talking to and investing in building relationships with producers who are 2 or 5 years in, not just 20 or 30 years in. (In reality you should do both, and later in the book I will show you how to do this.)

This can mean building relationships with screenwriters or even actors who are not perceived as "A"-list now but who nevertheless could potentially help you as an author at some point in the future by referring your work to agents or studios because they really like you and have a relationship with you. (Again, I will show you how to do this later in the book.)

Understanding the game is basically recognizing that you should be a nice and genuine (and talented) person who builds real relationships with others who are pursuing their dreams in entertainment just like you. Because Hollywood is run on relationships perhaps more than any industry in the world, making this your approach will be key to your success as our HERO.

Understanding What Winning A Game Looks Like

Finally, playing the game also consists of understanding what "winning" looks like.

The old definition of winning as an author in Hollywood, for example, was having your book or IP turned into a movie or television project. If that didn't happen, then, well, you were a loser. And nobody likes (or at least wants to associate with) a loser.

But this is a completely wrong definition.

Winning in the entertainment game is so much bigger than this simple (and backwards) notion that is peddled on the internet.

Winning consists not only of getting your work made, but so much more. In fact, there are various levels of winning in Hollywood but few ever tell authors (or people outside of the industry) this. (This is why there are some writers or producers who have made hundreds of thousands or millions of dollars in the system but who have never been "credited" for their work. These people are still winners even if the public doesn't know their name or their names aren't full of IMDB credits—and they are winners all because they understand how to win at the behind-the-scenes game.)

In a nutshell, winning in Hollywood consists of winning at "the process of Hollywood" (i.e., attempting to turn your book into a show or movie), not just winning in "the end result of Hollywood" (i.e., actually turning your book into a show or movie).

But why?

Because the process of winning in Hollywood is full of new knowledge, new contacts (and hopefully new friends), and new money (when your work is optioned, or rented, for a fee for a certain period of time for example).

Even if your IP isn't turned into a movie or television show in the short-term, you can still win. And any time you hit little victories in the process of turning your work into something more, you should celebrate it as a win because you will have grown as a person and professional; developed exciting new relationships; and (depending on your IP) made thousands or tens of thousands or hundreds of thousands of dollars off of simply renting (i.e., optioning) your work for a very short period of time.

Of course, I'm going to show you how to win beyond this but I wanted to emphasize that winning at the process of Hollywood should not be underestimated or overlooked. There are many people who have made entire careers off of winning at this process (and there are many authors just like you who have had substantial side-hustles off this process too). Knowing this information will make you a better player and HERO in this game because it will give you the right perspective going into it.

CHAPTER 3

SHOULD YOU TRY TO ADAPT YOUR OWN BOOK TO PITCH TO HOLLYWOOD?

> "The best advice I've ever gotten is to be yourself.
> Stay true to who you are."
>
> — *Snoop Dog*

Even with the right mindset and perspective about how to win in Hollywood, you might be asking yourself the following questions:

1. Should I write the screenplay for my novel (or IP) and adapt my own work when approaching Hollywood?
2. If I don't adapt my own work, can I really trust Hollywood to look at my story or do a good job with my creation?

Although these are the right questions to ask, they are a bit premature in terms of getting your story on the big or small screen—or even getting your story in front of agents, producers, or studio executives at this point. There is a process you must go through before this—developing a written treatment and/ or visual pitch deck, for example—that I will teach you how to do later in this book. But it is important that we address these questions around adaptation now so you can understand your role in the process or HERO's journey you are about to take.

Why Adapting Your Own IP Isn't Always A Great Idea

Let's tackle the first question. The answer to whether you should write the screenplay based on your own IP is "it depends." I know, I know: it seems like a copout. But in reality it isn't.

It depends because you truly might be one of the rare great writers who can write both novels AND write scripts.

The author who is perhaps the best example of this was Mario Puzo. For example, he wrote both the novel *The Godfather* as well as the screenplay for the movie *The Godfather*, for which he won an Academy Award for best adapted screenplay. (He also wrote the screenplay for the 1978 film *Superman*.)

But as far as author-screenwriters go, he is the exception and not the rule. That is, he is one of the only authors who was known to have the ability to operate in both mediums extremely well (a more recent example of a successful novelist-screenwriter is Gillian Flynn who adapted her own novel, *Gone Girl*, into a successful film).

But again, these are exceptions. But just because they are successful exceptions doesn't mean other authors haven't tried to adapt their own work too.

For example, the great novelist F. Scott Fitzgerald attempted to adapt his book *The Great Gatsby* for Hollywood but it ended in failure. The great screenwriter William Goldman— considered by many to be the greatest screenwriter to ever live—attempted to adapt one of his novels to a screenplay and he also failed. The same is true for the great Michael Chricton.

For example, Michael Chricton was the author of *Jurassic Park* among other beloved classics. But when he tried his hand at screenwriting—when he created the show *ER* and delivered the pilot script for Hollywood executives—industry insiders were grateful but perplexed. They were grateful that he would attempt to write the script but also perplexed because the script was about 100 pages longer than traditional TV format requirements. In his case, he wanted to eschew the standard format that networks and studios look for when developing shows and executives had to tear up the script and go back to square one.

The same is true for when the novelists like Agatha Christie, Margaret Atwood, William Faulkner, and John Steinbeck attempted to write screenplays—they didn't work out much to these novelists' chagrin.

Part of the reason for this is because of the inherently different formats for novels and scripts. If you have a novel, you have more time and space to develop rich worlds with big characters who have great backstories and inner-dialogue that can engage your readers in a meaningful way. In scripts, you unfortunately do not. And as a consequence it becomes a very painful process for "killing your baby" if you attempt to narrow your story, merge certain characters, cut important themes, and the like during your adaptation.

Again, I believe in you as the HERO that you are but it is a very difficult thing to try to do. If you do want to try your hand at it, I encourage you to because you just might also be the exception to the rule too. Just know that you might be met with skepticism or dismissiveness from industry insiders not because they don't believe in you, but because of the less than stellar history of authors being able to adapt their own work. In their minds—and business models—they will 9 times out of 10 neither ask nor expect you to adapt your own work. And if you ask them to adapt your own work, 9 times out of 10 they will tell you "no."

That said, you can always pen a script prior to approaching Hollywood (or writing your book) that insiders might be willing to read and eventually adapt. Author Ernest Cline who wrote the novel *Ready Player One* wrote the screenplay prior to writing the book version and as a consequence was able to also co-write the screenplay of the movie to great success (after Universal realized he could write in both mediums). (*Ready Player One* would go on to attach Steven Spielberg as director and make nearly $600 million dollars at the box office.)

Allowing Hollywood To Adapt Your Work

In most cases, though, Hollywood will want to assign a writer to adapt your work. This is true regardless of if you are traditionally published or independently published. This is true whether you are attempting to turn your work into a movie or television series. And this is true if you've sold one copy of your book or one hundred million copies.

Of course, not every author is happy with how screenwriters, producers, directors, actors, and studios end up interpreting their work for the screen. Authors behind the books that became movies like *I Am Legend, Willy Wonka & The Chocolate Factory, Mary Poppins,* and *Forrest Gump,* for example, all disliked their on-screen adaptations. (I won't repeat what some of them had to say about their on-screen adaptations either because, let's just say, they were quite indignant about them.)

On the other hand, though, the authors behind the books that became the films *Blade Runner, Fight Club, Crazy Rich Asians,* and *Hidden Figures,* among others, loved how their stories came to life in Hollywood and couldn't have been more pleased.

The key thing is recognizing that even when your work goes up on screen, there is no guarantee that you will love it or hate it. That will mostly depend on not only who is attached to write it, but also who directs it, stars in it, edits it, makes the costumes, scores it, and so on.

Because your story is going from being just your creation (as an author) to now hundreds or even thousands of people's creation (as a movie or television series), bringing it all together to make it work is much more complicated than many people realize. So long as you understand this—that you go from being a captain of a one person mini boat to being a private on a massive, military-like naval ship—it will help you as your book makes its way through the development and production process. (And if becoming a private on a larger ship doesn't sound enticing, know that there are significant financial and professional rewards to incentivize you like making the standard 2%-3% author's cut of a film's $10 million, $50 million, or $100 million dollar production budget as soon as it starts shooting.)

CHAPTER 4

THE 3 TYPES OF CONTRACTS HOLLYWOOD OFFERS AUTHORS

> "How can he find his own way if he does not learn
> to choose a path?"
>
> — *Life of Pi*

As our HERO, it is critically important to familiarize yourself with the types of agreements—or contracts—Hollywood will offer you prior to starting your entertainment journey. It's important to familiarize yourself so that you can:

1. Be more knowledgeable, avoid rookie mistakes, and capture more money for yourself in the process;
2. Understand the pros, cons, and playbook of the game you are about to enter;

   And 3) Mentally and emotionally prepare yourself for what could be an incredible roller coaster of a journey.

Simply put, your business mission as an author in Hollywood is to get a shopping agreement, option agreement, or purchase offer for your work. Nothing more. Nothing less.

I'll explain the differences between these things below because each agreement is as different from the other as casual dating, serious relationships, and marriages are different from one other.

Shopping Agreement

In the simplest terms, a shopping agreement is a standard agreement between yourself and a producer, agent, or manager who is excited about your book or other piece of IP and who wants the ability to "shop" (or pitch) your project around town for a specified period of time. The period of time is usually either 6-12 months, can be either exclusive or non-exclusive to them, and is basically like casual dating: it allows you to test out the producer's ability to sell and the producer to test out the strength of your IP without either party committing to a long-term relationship together.

A shopping agreement allows the producer, agent, or manager to present your project to potential financiers, studios, and networks, among others, without initially compensating you for your work. In other words, it allows them to shop your IP for free so that they don't have to spend any money upfront and so that you don't have to give up the rights to your creation (right away, at least).

The advantage to this approach for you is if your IP heats up and gets lots of interest, you can potentially get more money from a studio, network, or streamer because you have not pre-negotiated the purchase price of your IP. It allows you to negotiate directly with the potential buyer(s) (if you want to, though I would leave that to the entertainment lawyers) and it allows you to not leave any money on the table.

For example, let's say you agreed to allow a producer to shop your work for free through a shopping agreement instead of entering a deal where they "option" your work for, say, $10,000. If your work sells for $100,000 or $500,000 or $1,000,000, you get to keep most of this money with a shopping agreement.

Option Agreement

On the other hand, if you option (or rent) your work for $10,000 and your work sales for $100,000, $500,000, or $1,000,000, you would only keep your $10,000. In other words, you could be leaving lots of money on the table because you pre-negotiated a purchase price with an option agreement and could end up kicking yourself for it.

That said, that doesn't mean that you should automatically reject "option" agreements. Option agreements should actually be preferred if you can get them because most IP doesn't sell for a huge amount of money initially, so having a producer pay you upfront for the right to rent your work to pitch to studios, networks, and streamers is free money for you without you having to do much of anything. In addition to that, option agreements in Hollywood are up over 500% since the Covid-19 Pandemic so they are floating around everywhere.

Option agreements are usually 12-18 months in length and currently are going anywhere from $500 to $10,000. They give intellectual property rights to the producer during the term of the option period and give them the ability to freely negotiate with the studio for a purchase. In other words, option agreements are like getting into a serious relationship with a Sugar Momma or Sugar Daddy who wants to dole out money on you because they love the beauty of your package (i.e., your IP). But in exchange they are the boss and pretty much call the shots in your relationship.

Purchase Offer

Of course, entering either a shopping agreement or option agreement can take you to the same destination: ultimately getting a purchase offer for your work. When you do get a purchase offer from a studio, it usually means that as the author you will get 2%-3% of the gross fees of a film's overall production budget (with a cap, or ceiling, on what you can make). As mentioned in the last chapter, if a studio or network buys and then makes your IP, you could be in for a very handsome pay day.

In practical terms, if your IP becomes a movie and you get 2%-3% of a $10 million dollar film's production budget with a cap, you could be looking at around $200,000 to $300,000. If your IP becomes a cable or premium cable show, you are looking at around $25,000 to $50,000. And all of this money comes on the first day your project starts shooting (called "principal photography" in the industry).

That said, getting a purchase offer is a bit like being proposed to: if you say yes you are officially engaged (i.e., you and the studio want to make a project and have a beautiful future together), but that doesn't necessarily mean you are married yet (i.e., you and a studio haven't made a project together because there are still lots of things you need to figure out).

In other words, you are only married once you and the studio actually start making the movie, which is a much more complicated process called "development." But before discussing that, let's explore a bit more about the exact players who will help you sell your IP, the players they will sell them to, and what these players are looking for.

CHAPTER 5

THE HOLLYWOOD PLAYERS WHO WILL HELP YOU SELL YOUR BOOK

> "I'm not looking for the best players, I'm looking
> for the right ones."
>
> — *Miracle*

The Players Who Will Help Get Your Work Sold

Of the 600,000 people who work (mostly behind the scenes) in Hollywood, as an author you will only need to interact with a small number of them to be successful. Later in the book I will show you how to identify and reach out to these people, but for now let's take a look at their role so you will know exactly what they do—and why it takes so long and costs so much to make the movie or television series your book deserves to become.

But before diving into each player, the important thing to understand about them is they are people just like you and me— they are HEROS just like you and me. They have hopes, dreams, and goals. They have families. They have to pay rent and car payments. They are movie and television nerds. They moved to Los Angeles for their dreams, often struggled, and as underdogs overcame the odds against them. These people are just like you and me and are constantly looking for new people—new talent, new ideas, new friends—because that is what gives them their sense of purpose in life.

These players, contrary to popular opinion, are often very nice, friendly, and even approachable. Sure, the stories about diva stars or producers or studio execs are true, but that is only a tiny fraction of the otherwise very cool and relatable people who come from backgrounds and neighborhoods from all over the world.

I guess what I'm trying to say is there is nothing scary or intimidating about the people you are about to meet and work with in Hollywood. There is no need to exalt them or believe they have super powers. All you need to do is respect them, want what is genuinely best for them (and you), and go into the industry with a "team player" attitude. And when you do, word will get around very quickly that you are nice, easy to talk to and work with, and that you understand what's necessary to succeed—which is the foundation of a very successful run in Hollywood so many have had.

The First Door Into Hollywood: The Manager

Having said that, the first door you are likely to encounter in Hollywood is that of "The Manager." The Manager—or managers, if they are a team—are probably the most laid back people in the industry. They often work from their homes in their pajamas and are experts at not only spotting new talent, but also building great (and genuine) relationships.

The Manager typically will take 15%-20% of whatever earnings you make from your IP if you sign with them. This is true if you are a bestselling author or if you have only sold your book to your family and friends.

Because the lines in Hollywood are blurring, managers—even if they are relatively new or junior—often have direct access to studios, networks, and streamers and can pitch your project on your behalf. But please understand this: only managers, producers, or agents can take your work before other Hollywood decision makers. That is, unfortunately you cannot cold call, email, or otherwise reach out to a studio or network on your own because, legally, it puts both you and the studio or network in jeopardy if there is ever an intellectual property dispute.

Although there are IP disputes, for the most part most people in Hollywood are honest and ethical and will not steal your idea. They won't because if they do—and are caught—they could not only be held legally and financially responsible, but they could also lose their jobs and reputations and be unable to ever work again in the industry. And nobody wants to put themselves in that type of situation.

The Second Door Into Hollywood: The Producer

Another door that will allow you to break into Hollywood is by working with—or befriending— "The Producer." Although there are many different "types" of producers, the type I'm referring to is a business or creative producer who specializes in developing new IP, pitching it, and shepherding projects from idea to reality. (There are other types of producers who focus on other aspects of the business but you won't typically be working with them as an author.)

The Producer can come in all kinds of different personalities. Some are young and fun. Others are old and cranky. Some have one or two successful projects under their belt while others might have 30. Some operate as solo practitioners (very successfully) and others employ a small or large team of people to advance their projects (also very successfully).

But the important thing about producers to understand is that, just like you and me, they all have individual tastes, preferences, and the like—for how they like to work (on their own or overseeing a big team) and the type of art they like to make. One of my producing partners, Andrew Carlberg, for example, loves to make socially impactful films (and he's won an Academy Award for doing so). Another one of my producing partners, Kayona Brown, loves sports projects (and she's won an Emmy Award for doing so).

So every producer you meet will specialize in one or a few areas just like you, as an author, specialize in one or a few genres. So when approaching producers in Hollywood, the path of least resistance is to identify and reach out to producers who have similar tastes as you. The spark between you all could be electrifying.

The Third Door Into Hollywood: The Agent

A third door into Hollywood, although a bit more remote if you're just starting out, is "The Agent." Agents often wear suits, have aggressive and competitive personality types, and live for the ability to make a "deal."

That is, an agent will be able to look at your IP and know exactly the "right" talent (i.e., writers, directors, and actors) to make your film or television show with. They will go to bat for you—they will even go to war for you—and use every persuasion tool in their arsenal to see your work succeed. Agents can be some of the best people to advocate on your behalf as they typically have started at the very bottom in Hollywood (by literally delivering mail) and climbed their way up. They are the very definition of "hustler."

The big agencies in Hollywood include Creative Artist Agency, William Morris Endeavor, United Talent Agency, International Creative Management, and Gersh, among others, who represent celebrity talent and other industry "big names." Of course, there are also boutique agencies that specialize in representing high-caliber talent as well. And there are literally dozens of other agencies that represent people of varying degrees of success.

As an author, if you interact with an agent who likes your work they can also pitch it around town. But more likely, an agent will get involved AFTER a manager or producer attaches to your work and a studio has shown interest. Agents typically receive a 10% commission.

The Studio and Network Players, What They Do, & How They Advance Your Work

As mentioned above, only managers, producers, or agents have the ability to pitch your work. But the question is, who are they pitching it too?

There are two types of players these people will be pitching your work to: studios and networks. And within the studio and networks, they will be pitching to people referred to as "development executives."

Studios vs. Networks

Although it might seem like semantics, understanding the difference between a studio and network is important so you can understand why it takes so long and can be so complicated to see your work on screen.

Studios are usually the first stop managers, producers, or agents will take your work to pitch. In a nutshell, studios are the players that finance and own television shows and movie projects.

On the other hand, networks are usually the players who license (for a limited period of time) these shows and movies from the studios.

The reason a manager or producer will go to a studio first is because they have the money, physical space (i.e., sound stages), and operational history of being able to successfully make movies or television shows. So a manager or producer will approach a "development executive" at a studio and pitch them your project. A development executive's job is to hear new ideas (similar to Shark Tank), evaluate them based on a variety of factors, and say yay or nay to them.

In short, managers, producers, or agents often have very close relationships with studio development executives which makes it easy for them to call or e-mail these executives with new ideas like yours. It is similar to you having a good friend from school or work that you constantly talk to and do business with.

Once a studio gets on board to back your IP—after a back and forth process—your manager, producer, or agent will then approach the network. The network, like ABC, NBC, CBS, or Fox, also employs its own development executives who hear pitches from the studios. But if they like your project and agree to buy it, it is at this point you get a purchase offer.

Who The Buyers And Sellers Are

Hollywood's system of buying and selling shows and movies is as old as the industry itself. Even if new technologies and players have emerged to change the game, the development process for taking your IP and turning it into something for the big or small screen has remained the same.

Right now, there are currently 49 buyers (i.e., networks) who are actively looking for IP. If you turn on your television and flip through the channels, these will be the players (i.e., ABC, CBS, NBC, Disney, Netflix, etc.).

In general, every network, just like every author or producer, will have its own tastes and preferences. It will also have its own "programming strategy." That is, it will have its own target market of viewers it tries to appeal to. But as an author shopping your IP, just know your manager, producer, or agent will understand the programming strategies of each network and exactly who to pitch your work to.

Typically, your work will be pitched anywhere from 3 to 12 studios or networks or more. If it's children's content, it is less. For example, there are only 5 buyers of children's content (i.e., Disney, Nickelodeon, etc.) and your manager or producer will know this.

But in order to get your work in front of these buyers, you will need to not only know what they're looking for but also know how they are looking for it to be presented to them. Let's turn our attention to that next.

CHAPTER 6

SPECIFIC ITEMS HOLLYWOOD BUYERS ARE LOOKING FOR FROM YOU

"Give people what they want, then later you can give them what you want."

— *Big Night*

What Types of Shows Studio and Network Buyers Are Looking For

As previously mentioned in the book, what players (and buyers) are looking for is constantly changing. And if Hollywood is anything, it is a trend and fad machine.

But I don't mean this in a negative way. I mean this in the sense that players in Hollywood follow trends closely because they want to make the safest possible bets on projects they believe have the highest likelihood of success.

They do this not only for business and financial reasons, but they do this because if they make a bet on a wrong project that is going against the current fad and it fails it could potentially mean they lose their jobs. And unfortunately, it happens more than anyone would care to admit. To insiders, Hollywood is like a banking system and if the executives underwrite a risky investment that goes south—instead of a safer one that checks all of the boxes—the bank's president will show them the door.

This is why you, as our HERO, will want to do everything in your power to present your book or IP in the way that makes it as attractive as possible because you will make these executives' lives so much easier. The truth is they are secretly rooting for you (they really do want to discover the next big thing) and so you should provide them with as much firepower as possible so they can fight to buy your book to turn into a movie or television series.

Because Hollywood buyers hear countless pitches on a weekly basis, you'll want to be sure to do the following for your book or IP so that your manager, producer, or agent can give these buyers what they're craving on a silver platter. Now serving it to them on a silver platter doesn't guarantee they will eat it, but it makes it a whole lot likelier they will.

A Checklist To Give Buyers What They Want

1. You will want to create a cinematic logline for your buyer
2. You will want to choose the right "franchise type" for your buyer
3. And you will want to present your book or IP in a written and/or visual form in as compelling (and standardized) a way as possible for your buyer

Cinematic Logline

Now let's start with the first item on your checklist, the logline.

In a nutshell, a logline is a one or two sentence description of the person your story is about; what their goal is; and the obstacle that stands in their way. It is meant to be concise and intriguing, and is possibly the most important thing you can develop for buyers. It's so important because buyers will often decide whether they want to hear more about your book or IP just from hearing the logline alone.

Buyers do this not because they are superficial or lazy or don't want to give you the time of day; they do this because they are inundated with pitches, scripts, and other projects and need a quick way to decide whether to break away from their other tasks to give you a little more attention.

But they also do this because 9 times out of 10, a great logline means that the project probably has the other elements they are looking for too so they perk up quickly when something catches their attention. And again, they really are hoping something does catch their attention—they truly are rooting for you, our HERO, to give them something spectacular and amazing.

But the important thing to know as an author about giving buyers a logline that is spectacular and amazing is that it should be different from the "blurb" or description of your book. I repeat: your movie or television logline should be different from the blurb or description of your book.

Let's look at a couple of book-to-film examples—*Jurassic Park* and *The Hunger Games*—to help illustrate this point a bit further.

Jurassic Park Book "Blurb" vs. *Jurassic Park* Movie "Logline"

The beloved Michael Chricton novel, *Jurassic Park*, is not only a great book but it was also turned into a great movie. But the distinction between the book blurb used to sell to customers is very different from the movie logline used to sell to Hollywood buyers. Here they are for your perusal:

Jurassic Park book blurb:

"An astonishing technique for recovering and cloning dinosaur DNA has been discovered. Now humankind's most thrilling fantasies have come true. Creatures extinct for eons roam Jurassic Park with their awesome presence and profound mystery, and the world can visit them - for a price. Until something goes wrong…"

Now, the *Jurassic Park* movie logline:

"A pragmatic paleontologist visiting an almost complete theme park is tasked with protecting a couple of kids after a power failure causes the park's cloned dinosaurs to run loose."

Can you see the difference between the two? The book blurb is leisurely, the movie logline is fast-paced; the book blurb allows you to paint a picture with your imagination, the movie logline paints the picture for you; the book blurb is general, the movie logline is specific; the book blurb discusses the what, the movie logline discusses the who; the book blurb discusses no goals or obstacles; the movie logline succinctly discusses both goals and obstacles; the book blurb leaves you saying "this is interesting"; the movie logline leaves you screaming "I need to see this!"

Now, let's look at the book blurb and movie logline for *The Hunger Games* to make sure we really absorb this point.

The Hunger Games Book "Blurb" vs. *The Hunger Games* Movie "Logline"

The Hunger Games book blurb is:

"Winning means fame and fortune. Losing means certain death. The Hunger Games have begun...in the ruins of a place once known as North America now lies the nation of Panem, a shining Capitol surrounded by twelve outlying districts. The Capitol is harsh and cruel and keeps the other districts in line by forcing them to participate in the annual Hunger Games, a fight-to-the-death on live TV.

"One boy and one girl between the ages of twelve and sixteen are selected by lottery to play. The winner brings riches and favor to his or her district. But that is nothing compared to what the Capitol wins: one more year of fearful compliance with its rule.

"Sixteen-year-old Katniss Everdeen, who lives alone with her mother and younger sister, regards it as a death sentence when she is forced to represent her impoverished district in the Games. But Katniss has been close to dead before - and survival, for her, is second nation. Without really meaning to, she becomes a contender. But if she is to win, she will have to start making choices that weigh survival against humanity and life against love."

Now, compare this long-ish book blurb with *The Hunger Games's* movie logline:

"Katniss Everdeen voluntarily takes her younger sister's place in the Hunger Games: a televised competition in which two teenagers from each of the twelve districts of Panem are chosen at random to fight to the death."

Again, can you see the dramatic difference between this book's blurb and its movie logline? It all comes down to being able to succinctly and cinematically describe who your story is about, what they want, and what's stopping them from getting what they want in a way that is engaging and entertaining.

I know, I know: cutting the beauty of your words down to something as short as a sentence or two might be very challenging. But as our HERO, not only do I believe in your ability to do this but I believe in your ability to do this in a spectacular way. And when you do, you will be ready to take the next step: choosing the "franchise" that is best for your book or IP.

The Right "Franchise Type": Making Your Story a Movie vs. Making it a Television Series

Now, let's move to the next item on your checklist: your franchise.

A "franchise" in Hollywood can mean many things. The thing that comes to mind for most authors are franchise movies like *The Godfather* series, *Rocky* series, *The Fast & The Furious* series, and so on. These movies are simply a part of a movie brand featuring the same characters in many different installments.

But a franchise can also simply mean the format or delivery vehicle of your book. And this most often comes in the form of a movie or television series. That is, your franchise type is the format of your show (i.e., a movie or television series).

But how do you know which one is best for your book or IP?

The answer is simple: if you feel the characters, world, and story you have created should best be told as 1 story you have a movie on your hands. If you feel your story should best be told as 100 stories (or episodes), then you have a television series.

But the important thing here is not to "hope" or "force" your story into being a television series if it really is better as a movie. Or vice versa.

In general, books or IP about cops, lawyers, and doctors are better as television series because they have a "story engine" that can generate lots of different episodes (i.e., case of the week). Put differently books with story engines that can generate episode after episode, season after season, are best for television—which is why in television the "bosses" are the writers (not the directors or producers contrary to popular opinion) because writers need to be able to think of many different storylines from the world you've created. And this is what makes them so valuable (and literally in charge of the entire television system).

On the other hand, books that feature new worlds, exotic locations, characters with a dramatic arc, and closed endings might be better as movies.

Half Hour Comedy vs. One Hour Drama vs. 120 Minute Movie

Having said that, once you know which franchise (or format) your book is more suited for you will then want to narrow it down a bit further. If your book has comedic overtones like Candace Bushnell's book *Sex and the City* (which became a television series), for example, then it belongs in the "half hour comedy" television space. If your book is more of a drama like the show *Scandal* (which was inspired by a real life person and real life stories) it belongs in the "one hour drama" television space.

If your book is in either of these television spaces, you will want to (in addition to creating the logline):

1. Create an idea of (not screenplay for) what the pilot episode will be about
2. Create an idea of (not screenplay for) 4-6 potential season 1 episodes
3. Create an idea of (not detailed description for) what several potential seasons might look like

If your book is a 120 minute movie, you will want to (in addition to creating the logline):

1. Create an idea of (not screenplay for) what the story is about (a brief synopsis in other words)

I will show you how to do these things in the next couple of chapters on Hollywood "treatments" and pitch decks so you can present these ideas in a cinematic, compelling, and standard way (which is the third item on your checklist).

But before I show you how to do these things, please don't let all of this overwhelm you on your own HERO's journey. Whether you might be feeling like narrowing down your logline will be difficult or figuring out if your book should be a movie or television show, you can ask smart friends and family to help. At this point, you just want to start the process of refining your idea because, once it gets to your future manager or producer, they will help you refine it even further (so there is no need to panic and feel like you have to be perfect in this stage of the game—or in any stage of the game).

CHAPTER 7

HOW TO CREATE THE WRITTEN DOCUMENT YOU NEED TO GET IN THE DOOR

"Hollywood is a door leading to a
thousand doors."

— *Kensington Roth*

The third item in your author checklist is developing a treatment and/or pitch deck. (If you recall from the last chapter, the first two items on your author checklist included creating your cinematic logline and choosing your franchise type.)

In this chapter, we're going to take a look at developing a treatment for your book-as-film or book-as-television-series.

What Is A Treatment?

But at this point, you might be asking yourself what the heck is a treatment? Simply put, a treatment is:

1. A written pitch of your story (typically about a page long but sometimes 3-5 pages long) that...

2. Has an opening that hooks the reader, a closing that emotionally satisfies them, and…

3. That features your protagonist; central conflict; central emotional conflict; main and supporting characters; and the essential conflict/structure of your story

In many ways, you might be tempted to think that your treatment is a summary of your book. But it's actually a little more complicated than that. In reality, a treatment is more than and different from a summary.

Maybe the best way to describe a treatment is by comparing it to a great trailer: it offers your unique story concept; introduces you to the main characters; gives an overview of the tone and world; and provides those unforgettable moments that leave people screaming, "wow! I have to see this!"

In other words, a treatment is a "hype" document meant to get Hollywood players excited about backing your story.

To give you an emotional sense of what I mean, please check out the trailers on YouTube for the following films to understand just how much a short trailer can can give you goosebumps (just like short treatments can):

1. *Jaws* (1975)
2. *Terminator 2: Judgment Day* (1991)
3. *Goldeneye* (1995)
4. *Independence Day* (1996)
5. *The Matrix* (1999)

Now if you watched them, you will see that these trailers not only immediately intrigue you, but also give you a sense of who's involved, what emotional conflicts and tones the films are going to take, and leave you wanting to race to watch them. They are exciting, fun, dramatic, and most of all, cinematic.

You'll want to accomplish the same thing with your written treatment. Let's take a look at a real life example treatment from the movie *Mr. and Mrs Smith* (which wasn't based on a book but which nevertheless illustrates just how exciting you should make your treatment).

Movie Treatment Example

Mr. and Mrs. Smith Movie Treatment

Mr. & Mrs. Smith [Title]

Treatment for movie [Franchise Type]

By Simon Kinberg [Treatment Creator]

Based on the novel by [insert name] [a movie is "based on" a novel if it attempts to follow the novel faithfully]

Adapted from the novel by [insert name] [a movie is "adapted from" if it significantly changes the novel's characters or storyline]

Logline [your story's 1-2 sentence hook we learned about in the last chapter]

A bored married couple is surprised to learn that they are both assassins hired by competing agencies to kill each other.

Story [insert the highlights of Acts 1, 2, and 3 here with all their juicy twists and turns]

The plot starts with a bang. Literally. An assassin, JIMMY JACKSON, raids an FBI witness hideout. He blasts in, taking out Feds, wending his way straight to the target. Jimmy kills him, and heads out, but more Agents flood in—they chase and catch Jimmy red-handed, surrounded by bodies. And we cut from this fairly grisly scene to:

The totally clean, pristine kitchen in a suburban dream—the house in the glass bubble (the one god shakes to watch it snow). It's the Smith house. They're sitting down to dinner together, and it's clear this is a marriage without any life. They sit silent—don't even look at each other. You can hear the forks scrape the plates. A lot of tension. Then the phone rings. They go to separate rooms to take their calls. It's their offices—they both have to go into the city for emergencies at work. John says he needs to check inventory (at the plant), and Jane says she needs to fix a downed mainframe (at the office).

We see: John's office is actually a meat-packing plant in little Italy. And he's more alive here—in his element. His partner/contractor/best friend SAL tells him Jimmy Jackson was snatched by Feds. And now the boss wants Jimmy killed.

Meanwhile, way uptown, Jane's office is a sleek, high-tech corporate deluxe on the Upper East Side. She commandeers a team of associates (all female), who run this office with the latest software. Jane's friend JASMINE is second-in-command. She also got word on Jimmy—a highline contract on his head.

So... John and Jane draw this same target.

John and Jane meet back in the suburbs that night, at a party for their neighbors SUZY and MARTIN COLEMAN. At the party, we see John and Jane circulating in this world, becoming what this world expects—totally bland suburbanites. They watch each other—secretly annoyed, bored senseless by one another.

Back home, they climb into bed—opposite sides (no kiss goodnight, nothing between them), and go to sleep. The next morning, with birds chirping, John wakes up early and goes out to his toolshed in the yard. He peels back the floor, and climbs down into a secret compartment—filled with weapons. Jane wakes up, sees he's gone, and heads down to the kitchen, where there's a trick-wall in the oven—where she keeps her own arsenal. She pockets what she needs.

Jane drives away in her station-wagon, with a bumper sticker for the Neighborhood Watch. "Keeping our Streets Safe!" John and Jane both head off to their respective "business trips."

John and Jane's bosses want the same thing—they want Jimmy Jackson killed in a clean hit (no witnesses). Guarded by the FBI, he's no easy mark. As John and Jane prepare for the hit, it's clear they work with diametrically opposite styles:

Armed with an arsenal of hardware, John works moment-to- moment, on pure instinct and adrenaline, spontaneous, always on his toes, barrelling into hits head-on and gun-first.

On the other hand, Jane is a clean assassin, killing with meticulous stealth and strategy, relying on her support network of associates. Where John uses hardware, she uses digital software, drawing victims into traps, laying explosives. She maps every inch of her missions with flawless schematics—perfect precision, top-of-the-line surveillance, leaving absolutely nothing to chance. Her victims never even see her coming.

So, John and Jane separately track the target. In an intricate set-piece, they hit the target from opposite angles. But John and Jane get in each other's way. They attack one another, trying to get rid of the competition. With their faces covered, they don't recognize each other. They just barely manage to take out the target, and escape. As they disappear into the night, the FBI floods in.

John and Jane report their completed missions to their bosses...but they both know there's a problem: they left a witness at the hit—a witness that needs to be eliminated in order to "clean" the scene. So John and Jane must find and kill this witness (they must find and kill each other).

They try to figure out who the other assassin is. As with everything, they use totally opposite styles. John hits the streets—using street contacts like an old-school assassin.

And Jane goes high-tech: using satellite and surveillance cameras (eyes in the sky), piecing together footage from the hit. They both quickly begin to suspect the other killer is... their spouse. And they're both equally shocked, confused, reeling. They're not one-hundred-percent sure. But they're definitely going to find out…

John returns home, to find Jane waiting there. They're both on point—not knowing how much the other one knows. She brings out wine and food—a feast. As they make small talk, they don't take their eyes off each other, scrutinizing every little move (where before they wouldn't even look at each other). Everything is charged, loaded now. Jane hesitates before eating her dinner, and John suspects (in that beat)—it's poisoned. Their eyes lock, he senses the truth.

Now, you can both feel and see this story. It's exciting. It's dramatic. It's intriguing. It's conflict-laden and full of twists, turns, and unforgettable moments. And you, as our HERO, should do your best to make your own movie treatment as engaging and titillating as this—even if it is not an action movie or thriller, and even if you have to significantly change some elements from your book to make it "pop." Buyers will be looking for that special "IT" or "WOW" factor and you can give it to them.

Television Series Treatment Example

That said, a movie treatment is a little DIFFERENT from a television series treatment, also known as a "Series Bible." Although both a movie treatment and television series treatment have the same mission—to excite and persuade buyers to purchase your IP—they are executed a tad differently.

Whereas a movie treatment includes its logline and complete story, a television treatment includes:

1. An overview of the television series
2. Its setting and location
3. A brief description of your characters (who they are, what makes them tick, how they relate to each other, etc.)
4. A brief overview of the pilot
5. Future episode ideas
6. Possibly future seasonal arcs (if it is a serialized show)

Here is an example of a bible from a comedic animated television series I created, *Animal Therapy*.

Animal Therapy Half Hour Television Treatment

Animal Therapy [Title]

Treatment for Animated Half Hour Show [Franchise Type]

By Dr. Rob Carpenter (Treatment Creator)

Logline: A highly neurotic therapy owl provides sketchy advice to animals for their growing list of emotional problems.

Series Overview [provide a brief description of what your show is]

Animal Therapy is an episodic, animated, satirical comedy about various cuddly and curmudgeon animals recalling their secret animal encounters in highly questionable therapy sessions.

Each episode features a different animal with a different problem they bring to the animal therapists, led by the highly neurotic and narcissist Dr. Strange Owl, and his team: a divorced man-hating marriage and family counselor, Jebony, and a boy-obsessed hypnotist and animal astrology expert, Heidi.

In Animal Therapy, wild animals have built their own fully functioning city— "Beast Town"—to escape from the domesticated pets and people of nearby "PetVille" and all of their drama. (The domesticated pets in PetVille are the villainous alter-egos of the wild animals in Beast Town.)

No matter what problem animals have, Dr. Strange Owl and his team always have conflicting solutions—that *sometimes* work.

Setting [provide a brief description of the unique setting, location, or world of your series]

Animal Therapy is a dark, satirical comedy using animals as metaphors for the crazy issues facing individuals, pop culture, and society.

It explores the world of "Beast Town"—which has broken off from the domesticated pet and people world of nearby "PetVille"and all of their cute house and zoo pets. (PetVille features the villainous alter egos (aka "perfect pets") of the messed up animals in Beast Town.) Beast Town is a similar and exaggerated version of PetVille where animals can not only do everything both pets and people can do, but where animals experience crippling emotions (i.e., revenge, anxiety, and doubt, etc) and the pros and cons of living in today's messed up world.

It will have a visual style similar to *South Park* and *Legends of Chamberlain Heights*.

Characters [show the principal characters of your show, their uniqueness and flaws, their goal, and how they relate to each other]

The Principals

Dr. Strange Owl. Narcissistic and judgmental psychiatrist who saw "financial opportunity" to provide therapy for all these "crazy" animals. He is a cross between MTV's "Daria" and Family Guy's "Baby Stewie."

Author of books like "You Might Feel Skinny But You Look Fat," "Stop Acting Like a Little Tramp," and "Why I Married My Ex-Wife's Sister: A Memoir on Healing."

He worships his idol, LL Blue Jay, loves money, but secretly has a heart for "the little guy."

Heidi. Idealistic and naive hypnotist and animal astrology expert who is boy-obsessed and who never passes up a chance to hit on a client she finds attractive. She is like *Park & Rec's* "Leslie Knop/ Amy Pohler."

Heidi is highly educated - she went to Kale University - and she has a crush on the local dive bar owner, Gray Goose, and postal worker, Mail Chimp.

She suffers from anxiety and panic attacks, and has a hidden prescription drug addiction.

Divorced man-hating marriage and relationship counselor who likes to keep it real.

Jebony. Jebony is a "big mama" type—or Madea type—who is tough and tolerates no B.S. She feels the world discriminates against animals like her (she has a record) and believes in fighting the system.

She is mother to teenage son, Ripple, who is a real ladies man.

Gopher. Office assistant and overly ambitious intern. He is like "Ross Matthews" from *RuPaul's Drag Race*.

Loves sitting in on therapy sessions to be "entertained" and to "gossip" about them afterward with his mom.

Gopher constantly eats junk food and believes he is on the "fast track" to becoming an animal therapist himself one day.

Misha Strange Owl. Dr. Strange Owl's long-term girlfriend and baby mama who doesn't believe in "traditional marriage." She is like an animal version of "Miley Cyrus."

Misha is a former model and dancer turned social media star famous for her online videos featuring her ridiculously large booty.

She is the much younger sister of Dr. Strange Owl's ex-wife who struggles with society's expectations of her and raising a family. She also battles eating disorders.

Lil' Weasel. Lil' Weasel is the Mayor and Judge of Beast Town who institutes new rule that all laws and disputes get settled by rap battles.

He is Dr. Strange Owl's best friend who competes with him as the duo "The Lollipop Bois" in illegal underground street skate-offs in nearby PetVille. Lil Weasel co-owns the Grillz dental franchise and believes animals need to keep their mouth-care a little more flossy.

He is very charming, sneaky and unpredictable, and is simultaneously dating 4 hyena sisters—Kim, Kourtney, Klhoe, and Kylie—who fight over his lovin.

He is like the animal version of "Lil Wayne."

Overview of Pilot [provide a brief 3 or 4 paragraph description of the pilot episode]

The *Animal Therapy* pilot drops us straight into the world of human-free Beast Town, where MYLES (a monkey) unknowingly takes a high-end escort PICKLES (also a monkey) out on a date at the local bar, GRAY GOOSE. Pickles starts flirtatiously playing with all the other chimps' bananas at the bar which reveals she is a hooker, which the bar immediately starts roasting on Myles for, including bullying him on social media.

Myles is going crazy from all of the cyberbullying and wants to kill himself, so he goes to see the animal therapists who immediately disagree on the solution to help him: DR. STRANGE OWL offers him a packet of "Snoop Dogs" (marijuana to smoke) but he turns it down. HEIDI then recommends that Myles get his "chakras" cleansed to achieve peace within himself and uses a car vacuum to clear out his aura, but when that doesn't work, Dr. Strange Owl recommends the hiring of hit men—also known as the "MINI MEAN GIRLS"—to take out the cyberbullies permanently.

Meanwhile, Heidi develops feelings for Myles (and starts to awkwardly hit on him, but Myles is in love with Pickles) and Dr. Strange Owl's wife, MISHA, posts a controversial TwerkOut dance video online (featuring hyenas KIM, KOURTNEY, KHLOE, and KYLIE) that goes viral, for which she gets trolled online and hate mail.

The Mini Mean Girls take out Myles's bullies, Myles gets Pickles back, and Misha feels prouder than ever of her twerkout video.

Future Episode Concepts [list a few potential future episode concepts here]

Black Sheep. Parents of black sheep family in Beast Town, the Ebonys, feel like social outcasts and want to "dye their kids' wool white" to make life a little easier on them. Jebony prescribes watching "black media" (Barbershop, Soul Plane, & House Party) as a cure for their self hatred while Dr. Strange Owl encourages Heidi to embrace her "Jungle Fever" and newfound love of all things black. Zoe performs "Doesn't Matter If You're Black or White" for a local nightclub.

Stepford Wives. Dr. Strange Owl becomes obsessed with a group of competitive female show dogs from PetVille after he realizes how much money can be made in televised dog pageantry. Cougar convinces Heidi and Jebony to go on a double date with her clients, Jaguar and Mail Chimp. Dr. Strange Owl enjoys his new life and identity as the hot new dog pimp, "Uncle Poodle."

Justin Beaver. Justin Beaver cannot handle the pressure of his newfound fame in Beast Town. Zoe convinces her dad to convert their basement to "celebrity rehab house" to counsel Beaver, Snooop Dogg, LL Blue Jay, and others so she can meet artists and advance her music career. Gopher attempts to secretly record stars' therapy sessions and sell them to celebrity trash site TMZ (The Mammal Zone).

Moving Ahead

As you can see with my television series treatment/bible example, there is more detail you will want to provide if you are turning your book into a television show versus a movie so there is more homework for you to do here. And the reason for this is, as we learned earlier in the book, is because your book will have to be able to sustain upwards of 100 episodes or storylines—not just 1 storyline like a movie does.

Moreover, it is also important to note that for shows that are serialized (meaning you have to watch episode 1 to understand episode 2, and you have to watch episode 2 to understand episode 3 because they are all interconnected) you will want to include "arcs" for how each season will look. For example, in serialized shows like *Mad Men* or *Game of Thrones*, you will want to give a brief description for how season 1 might look, how season 2 might look, and so on AFTER you outline a few future episode concepts. And all this really means in practice is you will want to list in a few sentences on how season 1 will look compared to season two (i.e., major storylines for the seasons, how their themes change, twists and turns, etc.).

And voila, if you do these things this is how you create a movie or television treatment that can help you get in the door with the right managers, producers, or agents. It's really not magic at all; it's just rolling up your sleeves to make sure you include all of the right elements so you can get insiders to root for you and fight to bring your story, characters, and world to the screen.

But in addition to—or in replacement of—a treatment you can use to get you in the door you can also create a "pitch deck" that can be used as a selling tool too. We will turn our attention there next.

CHAPTER 8

HOW TO CREATE THE VISUAL DOCUMENT YOU NEED TO GET IN THE DOOR

> "Create your own visual style...let it be unique for
> yourself and yet identifiable to others."
>
> — *Orson Welles*

The wonderful thing about Hollywood is that there are lots of different ways to present your IP to get your foot in the door. One way, as we discussed in the last chapter, is by creating a written treatment for your book. However, another way that is frequently used is by creating a visual treatment—or pitch deck—of your work.

Even though either a written treatment or visual pitch deck can be effective, I recommend you have both in your arsenal. In my own life, for example, I was able to use a written treatment to convince insiders to back one of my projects but, for a separate project, I was able to use a pitch deck to convince a different group to support my work. In other words, when you have both documents you are putting yourself on more solid ground as you never know which one might be requested by insiders—or which one might work in your favor.

In another instance—when somebody who had both a pitch deck and written treatment approached me to produce their work— it made my life easier to quickly look through their documents to decide if I wanted to jump on board or not. (In case you're wondering, I did decide to produce their work (based on a book)—and I also decided to direct it.)

The Elements of a Pitch Deck

Just like a written treatment, a visual pitch deck follows a standard formula or format that buyers will be looking for. But more than anything else, they will be looking to see that this pitch deck is as visual and cinematic as possible so that it literally shows the tone, theme, and emotional blueprint of a story through images and colors and style.

In other words, your pitch deck is not just another powerpoint or just another presentation to stuff full of information. It is instead more like a lookbook that gives a small taste of what your story will look like on screen and so you will want to make it as pretty as possible. In other words, your pitch deck should be some pretty hot "eye candy" to look at.

But before you get nervous and wonder how you might be able to create a pitch deck especially if you're not a designer, don't worry. In my companion course to this book (Books to Big Screen), I provide editable templates you can use to make your life a lot simpler (and to reduce any fear or anxiety you might have about getting the pitch deck you need to move forward). I even have my own designers who can help create a custom presentation for you without breaking the bank if you're looking for something more specialized.

The important thing to understand, though, is that like anything else a pitch deck has certains standard elements to include that insiders will be looking for. They are:

1. A stunning cover page that includes the name of the movie or show
2. Your movie or show's logline
3. The synopsis of your show or movie
4. The world of your show or movie
5. The tone of your show or movie
6. Shows your show or movie is similar to
7. Visual representation of your characters (including with actor images)
8. Your show pilot or movie overview
9. Your show's future episode concepts (if it is a television series)
10. Your contact information

With pitch decks, you will want to keep them relatively brief. Anywhere from 10-20 slides is probably going to be your sweet spot. You will also want to make sure they are not "too wordy" or verbose, and keep them as understandable as possible. That is, you don't want to overwhelm readers with too much information that can become a distraction.

An example that might help give you a better grasp on what a pitch deck looks like in real life is at the web link below. It is from my animated comedic television series Animal Therapy.

Animal Therapy Pitch Deck Example

Animal Therapy Pitch Deck Example—please go to www.bookfunnel.com to download a free copy of the pitch deck.

CHAPTER 9

SPECIFIC WAYS TO REACH HOLLYWOOD PRODUCERS, MANAGERS, & AGENTS AS AN AUTHOR

"The seed that we planted in this man's mind may change everything."

— Inception

Now that we've covered the various elements you will need to approach busy insiders looking for books and IP just like yours, let's dive into how you can reach these busy insiders.

One of the biggest questions I hear from authors is "how can I find and get in touch with producers, agents, and studios?" "Where can I go to meet them?" How can I take that crucial first, second, and third step to break in?"

Although there is no singular path in—especially for a HERO like you who has many possibilities—there are a few tried and true approaches that can help you get in front of the right people. (These approaches work whether you are a traditionally or independently published author; but if you are traditionally published, be sure to check in first with your publisher and see if you can get in touch with your "media rights agent" to see if they will help navigate this process for you.)

Your College's Alumni Network

Maybe the first—and least obvious—place to search for Hollywood contacts is through your college's alumni network (if you went to college). Even if you didn't have a film school at your university (or even if it wasn't a very big one), you can call or e-mail your alumni network and ask who became managers, producers, or agents in Hollywood that you might be able to get in touch with.

Many times because Hollywood insiders have such an affinity for their alma mater, they would be willing to 1) take your call or email and/or 2) refer you to a colleague who would take your call or email. Of course, when you approach them you want to play up your angle and connection to the school as it will establish commonality with them which is a huge plus.

Your City's Film Community

Another way to reach out is through your local film community. Even if you're not local to Los Angeles, you can still take advantage of the connections closest to you as they might end up being the most helpful.

For example, in my experience most of the people I've ever come across in Hollywood are not from Hollywood and as a consequence many of them have a deep affection for people from their hometowns or communities who are looking to break in.

What this means for you is that you can research to see who's from where you're from and attempt to get in touch.

There are several practical ways to do this:

1. You can simply go to Google and search "Hollywood producers from [insert your community]"; you can also do the same for search terms like "Hollywood agents from" or "Hollywood executives from" and so on. If you get creative here, you might be surprised at what you find. And once you find these people, ask around enough to see where they went to school and who might know them from your community that you also know that can introduce you.

2. Depending on how big your community is—and depending on how big the Hollywood insider is—you can also go to your city or town's "Wikipedia" page. When you do, there should be a list of "notable people" and the Hollywood contact's name might be on there. If it is, use the same approach of seeing who you know that might know them.

3. You can also go to local film "meetups" or local film festivals and meet local producers and filmmakers who might have connections to Hollywood—or who might be able to help you themselves. You can use "Meetup.com" to search for film group's or festivals in your area that you can attend to start networking. But the key here is to not just go once; go a few times, make yourself known, and build relationships with people who can help get your foot in the door.

Regional, National, and International Film Festivals and Film Marketplaces

A third way to contact people is by going to regional, national, or international film festivals and marketplaces. A film festival usually features independent films (and the primary players who made them) whereas film marketplaces are usually places where films and/or movie concepts are bought from financiers. (An example of a film festival is Sundance and an example of a film marketplace is the American Film Market.)

But the key thing to understand here is that there are literally thousands of film festivals and dozens of film marketplaces that take place every year. You can meet countless people in entertainment by going to some of them and putting yourself out there. If you use this link you can see a comprehensive list of film festivals:

https://www.nyfa.edu/student-resources/film-festivals/

Here is a list of film marketplaces:

https://magdaolchawska.com/film-markets-around-world/

IMDB Pro

A fourth way to approach Hollywood insiders is through IMDB Pro. Now, the IMDB Pro version is different from the normal IMDB you might be familiar with that shows completed television and movie projects actors, directors, producers, and other insiders have worked on. In the Pro version, it is a paid monthly or annual subscription that also gives you access to the contact information of managers, agents, producers, and production companies and the type of current and upcoming projects they are working on.

But a word of caution here: just because you have access to these people doesn't mean you should spam them. Like with Hollywood alumni from your school or Hollywood insiders from your community, do a little bit of research to see who you know that might know them and would be willing to provide an introduction (and please be sure that the people you are trying to reach do projects in your genre and format type). Now, this might take some time but it'll be more advantageous to you to get an introduction if you can.

That said, if you can't find somebody to introduce you can call the production companies (and not the producers directly) and ask if "they are currently accepting new material." They might say yes or they might say no, but the key is to be gracious, non-demanding, and to respect whatever they say. In the event that they say no or only accept material from "managers" or "agents" (which is many production companies) try to get in touch with managers or agents through IMDB Pro using the same approach.

Local Production Websites

Like with IMDB Pro, there are other websites you can use that will have the contact information of managers, agents, and producers. The main (free) one for Hollywood is https://la411.com/ that lists thousands of companies you can reach out to. As an author or IP rights holder, you will want to reach out to "production companies" (and not, for example, "post production companies" or "grip and lighting equipment companies," etc. because those types of companies do not develop material like yours even though they are in the entertainment industry).

There are also local production websites in prominent film locations like Georgia, New Orleans, Toronto, London, and elsewhere that you can use to contact entertainment companies. Here are a few below:

Georgia:
https://www.productionhub.com/directory/profiles/film-production-companies/us/georgia

New Orleans:
https://www.productionhub.com/directory/profiles/film-production-companies/us/louisiana/new-orleans

Toronto:
https://www.productionhub.com/directory/profiles/film-production-companies/ca/ontario/toronto

London:
https://filmlondon.org.uk/resource/production-companies

How To E-mail Producers and Managers

Once you do get an introduction to a producer, manager, or agent—or once you have their contact information—you'll want to communicate with them in as clear and concise a way as possible. Even though they are looking for the next great project like yours, they are swamped and appreciate brevity.

In practice, it can look like the sample e-mail below:

Subject: Author with IP for new potential television series (or movie)

Dear Producer/Manager/Agent,

I very much enjoyed watching [insert a recent movie or television series they produced] and I was writing because I have a similar project you might be interested in. I am the author of [insert your book as a hyperlink to your Amazon sales page] which has built up an avid and passionate fan base, and which could be strong IP to base a movie or television series on. I have attached a written treatment and pitch deck for your review.

Hope you are well and to hear from you soon if you are interested in speaking further.

Respectfully yours,
Your name

As you can see, this e-mail is short and sweet. It establishes that you are familiar with the way Hollywood insiders work (which they will like); gives them a quick opportunity to check out your sales page (if you have a book); shows that there are die hard fans of your week (without necessarily saying it is a bestseller or not); and that you are not only open to having it optioned, but that you have done your homework by giving them your book (or IP) in standard movie or television format so they can quickly review it. Overall, it's a big win.

How to Call Producers and Managers

But if you only have a phone number, you can also reach out and see if a manager or production company is open to receiving new material. Here is a sample script you can use:

Hi, my name is [insert your name], I'm an author, and I was wondering if you are currently receiving new outside material and, if you are, what the best e-mail is to send it to?

If they say yes and provide an e-mail address, tell them thank you and send off an e-mail. On the other hand, if they are not receiving new material at this time, ask them if they will be in the future and when would be the best time to follow up. If they say they don't know or that they won't be, just thank them for their time and wish them a great day (no need to argue or try to persuade them, just simply to be gracious). And then move on to the next name on your Hollywood list.

Putting Things in Perspective

But remember, this process is all very doable for you HERO. It might take some research, time, and outreach to get somebody to sign off on bringing your story to the big or small screen, but all you need is one yes. There are literally thousands of producers, production companies, managers, and agents, and somebody is likely to want to provide you with a shopping agreement, option, or purchase offer. And even if they don't right away—or at all— just know that you can always repeat this process with your next book or piece of IP and try again.

As we discussed earlier in the book, Hollywood is full of people whose fortunes (and misfortunes) are constantly changing so if you are committed to playing the long game you will increase your likelihood of success.

CHAPTER 10

YOUR NEXT STEP AS AN AUTHOR

> "Find the ones who haven't given up.
> They're the future."
>
> — *Tomorrowland*

Congratulations! You've made it to the end of this short book and to the beginning of your future in Hollywood. I hope the information provided in this book has been useful to you and to hear about all of your upcoming success in show biz.

If you want to learn even more about how to turn your book or IP into a movie or television series, I have a couple of additional opportunities for you that you might be interested in.

The first is that I have created a companion online e-course, Books To Big Screen, that:

- Outlines the principles and strategies in this book even further

- Provides in-depth video interviews of Hollywood insiders looking to help you take the next step

- Provides editable templates for your written treatment
- Provides editable templates for your visual pitch deck
- Gives you feedback on if your work and a consulting session from me or my team
- Gives you the opportunity to upload and pitch your treatment/pitch deck to producers, managers, agents, and studios who are currently looking to option and buy IP

The second opportunity that I have created for you if you want to accelerate your progress and connect directly with Hollywood insiders is:

- Me or my team directly creating your written treatment AND pitch deck
- And the opportunity to directly pitch your book or IP to Hollywood insiders, including managers, agents, and Academy and Emmy award winning producers

If either of these things sound up your alley, please visit bookstobigscreen.com to learn more. Thank you again for taking the time to read this book and I wish you nothing but the best you, HERO, you!

WHAT HAPPENS AFTER YOUR BOOK IS OPTIONED OR SOLD

> *"You only get one life. It's actually your duty to live it as fully as possible."*
>
> — *Me Before You*

Without a shadow of a doubt, having your book or IP optioned or sold is one of the most exciting professional experiences you can have in life. It not only provides validation that one of the most competitive industries in the world believes in you, but it also gives you real potential to see your story on screen—a dream that millions of authors have had.

That said, many authors who go through this process also wonder what happens AFTER they have optioned or sold their work. After all, they may have heard—just like you have—that Hollywood projects can take "years" or even "decades" to produce (if at all) and might think to themselves WHY?

The answer to this question is a process called "development hell," or Hollywood lingo for insider politics, scheduling craziness, and coalition building your book or IP must successfully go through before it makes it on air.

Perhaps the best way to describe this madness is to showcase the process for what happens when you get an option as well as the process for when you sell your project.

What Happens When Your Book or IP is Optioned

In a nutshell, this is what happens when your book is optioned by a producer or production company:

- You typically sign an option agreement for 12-18 months and receive your option payment
- The producer or production company will refine your treatment or pitch deck to make sure it is aligned with their vision
- The producer or production company you have signed with then begins a very political process called "packaging"
- Packaging is when the producer or production company begins identifying other Hollywood insiders they can attach to the project to make it more "attractive" for a studio to buy
- In packaging, producers will attach a screenwriter to adapt your work and sometimes a top director, a top actor (if they can get them), or any number of other people if necessary
- Once the producer builds the "team," they will then "shop" your project to their network of contacts at studios to get feedback

- If they feel confident enough on the initial feedback, they will arrange a formal pitch of the project (and the pitch is usually given by the screenwriter they have attached who has already adapted your work or who will adapt your work)
- If the studio buys it, it then goes through a whole new process of refinements, attachments, and so on

What Happens When Your Book or IP is Sold

When your work is sold, it is a day of celebration but also a day that signifies another layer of development it must go through. In a nutshell, this is what happens after the incredibly exciting purchase offer from a studio:

- The producer or production company evaluates if the offer makes sense and accepts or declines it (in some cases, multiple offers are presented and bidding wars occur over your work). It will be the producer and not the author who makes this decision because the author has already legally licensed away their IP and negotiating rights.
- If the producer accepts an offer, then the studio begins its process of building the movie script or pilot script (and you get a check for selling your IP rights if you've negotiated properly)
- The movie script or pilot script will go through 6-12 drafts before the studio president personally signs off (or declines to sign off) on the script
- During the time the drafts are being written, it is not uncommon for multiple screenwriters to be hired, fired, and then re-hired to get the script where it needs to be

- If the studio president signs off on the final version of the script, then it begins a process called "pre-production"
- In pre-production, auditions begin for key cast; crew members are hired; filming locations are scouted and arranged; and other production elements are handled to begin shooting
- Once your project begins filming, you get another check (usually 2-3% of the production's filming budget, and capped at a certain amount)
- The project films over the course of 2-3 months (if it is a movie) or 2-4 weeks (if it is a television pilot)
- The project is then edited for a few weeks (if it is a television pilot) or 8-12 months (if it is a movie)—during which time multiple "cuts" or versions of the film are presented to the studio for refinement
- Once the project is complete, it will debut in its predetermined release time and location if it is a movie; if it is a television pilot, it will be shown to the studio and network who will then make a decision as to whether they will allow the project to air or if they will ultimately terminate it

Putting It In Perspective

As you can see, there is a long process that occurs after your book is optioned or sold. And during this process, your producer will deal with many different types of issues like egos (from executives, screenwriters, actors, directors, and more); creative pitches from writers and the studio; budgeting the shoot properly and financial crises if they go over budget; scheduling conflicts if actors or directors commit to the project and then back out; possible changes in executive leadership at the studio; and more.

To top all of this off, the producer will possibly be dealing with 4 or 5 of these projects simultaneously—and the studio your work is sold to will be dealing with dozens or hundreds of these projects at any one time as well.

The good news is that you, as our author HERO, do not have to put up with any of this yourself. You can be free to enjoy the fruits of your option or sale and leverage that for your next project. On the other hand, though, you may not be updated on the day-to-day politics of your project and what's going on with it, which could leave you feeling a little bit in the dark. But that's OK because it is just part of the process and something almost every author goes through when their book is turned into a movie or television show.

Of course, I've simplified much of this but this gives you the general idea of the behind-the-scenes of what is going on and why it may take years or even decades to get your work on screen. But if you can accept that this is how the sausage gets made—and summon all of the patience within you—you could be in for an incredibly rewarding ride.

AUTHOR ROADMAP

10 Steps To Turn Your Book Into A Television Series or Movie

1. Write your book, publish it, and build its audience
2. Create written treatment and pitch deck based on your book
3. Research producers, managers, and agents who might want to help who make movies and television shows in the genre your book is in.
4. Reach out to insiders with your treatment and pitch deck to secure interest and/or involvement.
5. Secure deal for shopping agreement, option agreement, or purchase agreement (be sure to have entertainment attorney look over your deal)
6. Get paid (first for the option agreement first and second for the purchase agreement)
7. Wait patiently until your project gets made
8. Leverage your book for your professional career
9. Enjoy the spoils of seeing your work come to screen
10. Repeat with any and all books or IP you would like

BOOKS TO BIG SCREEN

Books to Big Screen is the official e-course that brings the principals of *Red Carpet Manuscript* to life.

Jump in as Dr. Rob guides you through the step-by-step process for how to turn you book into a major Hollywood television series or feature film, and also helps connect you to the insiders to do it. In addition to an in depth look at the topics covered in *Red Carpet Manuscript*, you will gain access to video interviews with Hollywood insiders, Emmy Winners, Producers and Agents and an exclusive Facebook group for real-time advice from Dr. Rob. Once you've completed the Books To Big Screen course you are given the opportunity to book a strategy session with a Books To Big Screen team member to analyze your Logline, Treatment, Pitch Deck and Create an Action Plan to pitch your book.

You don't need to spend years in Hollywood or pay $100,000 for film school to access the tools you need to succeed in Hollywood. We guide you through step by step in an easy-to-understand way so that you'll know exactly what you need to do to get your book to the big (or small) screen - without being a bestselling author or knowing anyone in Tinseltown.

Visit www.BooksToBigScreen.com to learn more.

WORKS CITED

Brady, T. 2019. Gemini Man: How Will Smith Shed 25 Years For His New Film. Accessed from: https://www.irishtimes.com/culture/film/gemini-man-how-will-smith-shed-25-years-for-his-new-film-1.4036116#:~:text=%E2%80%9CWell%2C%20he's%20a%20very%20busy,that%20gets%20the%20movie%20made.

Conradt, S. 2017. 11 Authors Who Hated the Movie Versions of Their Books. Accessed from: https://www.mentalfloss.com/article/31001/11-authors-who-hated-movie-versions-their-books

Creamer, J. 2020. Global Content Spend Hit Record High of $220 bn in 2020. Accessed from: https://www.televisual.com/news/global-content-spend-hit-record-high-of-220bn-in-2020/

Gussow, M. 1999. Author Who Made 'The Godfather' a World Addiction, is Dead at 78. Accessed from: https://www.nytimes.com/1999/07/03/movies/mario-puzo-author-who-made-the-godfather-a-world-addiction-is-dead-at-78.html#:~:text=While%20writing%20the%20screenplays%20for,his%20career%20as%20a%20novelist.

Indie Wire. 2013. 12 Celebrated Novelists-Turned-Screenwriters And How They Fared. Accessed from: https://www.indiewire.com/2013/10/12-celebrated-novelists-turned-screenwriters-and-how-they-fared-248958/

Marlow, J. 2012. Make Your Story A Movie: Adapting Your Book or Idea for Hollywood.

Perez, L. 2019. Gillian Flynn Reflects on 'Gone Girl' Legacy and the Growing Appetite for Anti-Heroine Books. Accessed from: https://www.hollywoodreporter.com/news/general-news/gillian-flynn-reflects-gone-girl-legacy-rise-anti-heroines-1260003/

Pugliese, J. 2015. The Uncensored, Epic, Never-Told Story Behind 'Mad Men.' Accessed from: https://www.hollywoodreporter.com/news/general-news/mad-men-uncensored-epic-never-780101/

Rothwell, H. 2019. The Success of Book To Film Adaptations. Accessed from: https://medium.com/publishing-in-the-digital-age/book-to-film-adaptations-caec7c65e96a#:~:text=An%20incredible%2070%25%20of%20the,popular%20culture%20must%20be%20followed.

Rowley, J. 2021. 18 Authors Who Loved The Movie Adaptations of Their Books. Accessed from: https://www.ranker.com/list/authors-who-loved-movie-adaptations-of-their-books/jim-rowley

Saba, V. 2021. The Rise of Must-Read TV. Accessed from: https://www.theatlantic.com/culture/archive/2021/07/tv-adaptations-fiction/619442/

ABOUT DR. ROB

D r. Rob Carpenter—known simply as Dr. Rob—miraculously survived a tragic accident and vowed to not only rebuild his life, but to help other people rebuild their lives too. He has become a transformational author, filmmaker, and CEO who now advises professional athletes, celebrities, business titans, and everyday people on how they can become the best versions of themselves. Dr. Rob has been featured in *The New York Times*, *Business Insider*, and *People Magazine*; has been a former professor and filmmaker at the 2x Emmy Award Winning USC Media Institute for Social Change; and is the incoming on-air host of *The Great Health Debates* (formerly Harvard Health TV). He founded the School of Happiness which he presents around the world and has countless resources available on his website DrRob.TV to help uplift you— and to help uplift humanity. Dr. Rob is the first in his family to graduate from college.

BOOKS BY DR. ROB

The 48 Laws of Happiness: Secrets Revealed For Becoming The Happiest You

Red Carpet Manuscript: How Authors Can Bring Their Book To The Big Screen

www.ingramcontent.com/pod-product-compliance
Lightning Source LLC
Chambersburg PA
CBHW070842050426
42452CB00011B/2380